CELEBRITY BIOS

Hayden Christensen

Katherine Friedman

Children's Press®
A Division of Scholastic Inc.
New York / Toronto / London / Auckland / Sydney
Mexico City / New Delhi / Hong Kong
Danbury, Connecticut

Book Design: Michelle Innes
Contributing Editor: Eric Fein

Photo Credits: Cover, pp. 9–10, 12, 14, 20, 22, 24, 26, 29, 32 © The Everett Collection; p. 4 © Globe Photos; p. 7 © Kevin R. Morris/CORBIS; p. 17, 19 © Reuters NewMedia Inc./CORBIS; pp. 30-31 © CORBIS; pp. 34, 38 © AP/Wide World Photos

Library of Congress Cataloging-in-Publication Data

Friedman, Katherine.
Hayden Christensen / by Katherine Friedman.
    p. cm. -- (Celebrity bios)
Includes index.
Summary: Profiles the Canadian actor who was chosen to portray Anakin Skywalker in Episodes II and III of the *Star Wars* film series.
    ISBN 0-516-23907-4 (lib. bdg.) -- ISBN 0-516-23481-1 (pbk.)
    1. Christensen, Hayden, 1981---Juvenile literature. 2. Motion picture actors and actresses--Canada--Biography--Juvenile literature.
[1. Christensen, Hayden, 1981– 2. Actors and actresses.] I. Title. II. Series.

PN2308.C54 F75 2002
791.43'028'092--dc21
[B]
                              2001047267

Copyright © 2002 by Rosen Book Works, Inc.
All rights reserved. Published simultaneously in Canada.
Printed in the United States of America.
1 2 3 4 5 6 7 8 9 10 R 11 10 09 08 07 06 05 04 03 02

CONTENTS

1	Becoming an Actor	5
2	A Dream Come True	13
3	What the Future Holds	33
	Timeline	40
	Fact Sheet	42
	New Words	43
	For Further Reading	45
	Resources	46
	Index	47
	About the Author	48

CHAPTER ONE

Becoming an Actor

"I love acting because it's a bit of an escape. It gives you the ability to reinvent yourself. They say that acting is the shy man's revenge."
—Hayden Christensen on *starwars.com*

Hayden Christensen is on his way to becoming one of Hollywood's hottest young stars. His wholesome good looks and acting talent have put him in the spotlight. Now, he is facing his biggest acting challenge yet. Hayden will play Anakin Skywalker in *Episodes II* and *III* of the *Star Wars* saga. There is no doubt that this

When it comes to acting, Hayden keeps his cool.

HAYDEN CHRISTENSEN

young actor is going to give a performance that is out of this world.

GROWING UP

Hayden Christensen was born in Vancouver, Canada, on April 19, 1981. His parents are Alie and David Christensen. He has a close relationship with his parents, who are both in the communications business. In fact, he told *Entertainment Weekly* that one of his biggest turn-offs is "people who rag on their parents." He says his folks have always supported him.

Hayden also has a strong bond with his three siblings. He has an older brother, Tove, an older sister, Hejsa, and a younger sister, Kaylen. The siblings enjoyed a happy childhood. Their days were filled with sports, video games, music, and of course, *Star Wars*. "My brother Tove and I have always been big fans," Hayden said on *starwars.com*. "We used to play some of the early [*Star Wars*] video games

Becoming an Actor

Hayden's birthplace, Vancouver, is just north of the U.S. border and Washington State.

religiously, for an hour at a time, to make sure we became Jedi Knights."

Hayden got his first break with a little help from his sister Hejsa. As a young girl, Hejsa was a Junior World Trampoline Champion and appeared in a commercial for Pringles potato chips. One day, she went to meet with a talent agent. "There was no one to baby-sit me, [so] I

HAYDEN CHRISTENSEN

> **Did you know?**
> Hayden and his brother Tove have their own film production company, Forest Park Pictures. They plan to make many movies together.

went along for the ride...they asked me if I wanted to do some commercials, and I said sure," Hayden told *starwars.com*. So, at the age of seven, Hayden began acting in commercials.

From commercials he moved onto television shows. His first big break came in 1994 at the age of twelve. He played Skip McDeere on "Family Passions," a Canadian soap opera. He got his first movie role in 1995. It was a small role in John Carpenter's *In the Mouth of Madness*.

Hayden also landed roles in television movies. He acted in *Trapped in a Purple Haze*, Danielle Steele's *No Greater Love*, and *Freefall*.

Becoming an Actor

The "Higher Ground" cast (from left to right):
Kandyse McClure, Meghan Ory, Jewel Staite, Hayden
Christensen, Jorge Vargas, A.J. Cook, and Kyle Downes.

In 1999, he got another small movie role in *The Virgin Suicides*. The movie starred teen celebrity Kirsten Dunst. It was directed by Sofia Coppola, the daughter of famed director Francis Ford Coppola. Hayden also landed his first starring role in 1999. He was cast in the Fox Family Channel drama series "Higher Ground."

HAYDEN CHRISTENSEN

Hayden polishes his acting skills with A.J. Cook in a scene from "Higher Ground."

"Higher Ground" gave Hayden a good opportunity to work on his acting skills. He played the character Scott Barringer. Scott is a troubled high school football star who is sent to the Mt. Horizon School. At Mt. Horizon, students learn how to cope with their problems. The show is set in the Pacific Northwest and stars Joe Lando as the school's headmaster, Peter Scarbrow. Lando previously

Becoming an Actor

co-starred with Jane Seymour in the CBS TV series "Dr. Quinn, Medicine Woman."

Co-starring on the show with Hayden was A.J. Cook. A.J. played Shelby Merrick, another student at Mt. Horizon. A.J. and Hayden became good friends while making the series. A.J. could tell that Hayden was destined for bigger things. She told the *Toronto Sun*, "The fan mail that we get on the show for Hayden is, like, insane. All the girls are just so-o-o in love with Hayden. I get e-mails too, [asking], 'What's it like working with Hayden?' It's just so cute. It's so funny."

Once Hayden started working in prime-time television, doors began to open. "Higher Ground" premiered in January 2000. It got mixed reviews but people liked Hayden. The series ran for only one season, but that was enough to get Hayden noticed by some very "*force*-ful" people, who would change the course of his life forever!

CHAPTER TWO

A Dream Come True

"It's the most fun I've ever had in my life. And to be honest, it was heavier than I expected."
—Hayden in *Entertainment Weekly,* **on getting to use his very own lightsaber**

On May 12, 2000, the official *Star Wars* Web site made an announcement that would affect Hayden's future. Hayden had been chosen from over four hundred actors to play the lead role of Anakin Skywalker in *Episodes II* and *III*. These films are part of the *Star Wars* prequel trilogy. The first prequel film was *Star Wars Episode I: The Phantom Menace.*

Hayden will be facing an *Attack of the Clones* in his first *Star Wars* movie.

HAYDEN CHRISTENSEN

Jake Lloyd played Anakin Skywalker in
Star Wars Episode I: The Phantom Menace.

A Dream Come True

In the prequel films, Anakin Skywalker is a young Jedi Knight learning the ways of the Force. But he is destined to lose his way, turning to the dark side of the Force. As *Star Wars* fans know, Anakin Skywalker becomes Darth Vader.

THE SEARCH FOR ANAKIN

The search for the actor to play Anakin Skywalker took close to a year. During that time, *Star Wars* casting director Robin Gurland met with or viewed videotapes of 442 actors. Robin explained the search process to *starwars.com*: "There were no auditions; everything was done by meetings. It was basically sitting down for twenty minutes to two hours and finding out who they are as an actor and what kind of experience they have."

From that large group, Robin selected twenty-five actors and showed their tapes to *Star Wars* creator and director George Lucas. After Lucas watched the tapes, he met with

HAYDEN CHRISTENSEN

about ten of the actors. Of those, four actors were selected to audition in person for Lucas.

Each of the four actors did a screen test at Lucas's Skywalker Ranch. These tests were done with Natalie Portman, who plays Queen Amidala in the prequel films. "It was really a very relaxed situation," Robin told *starwars.com*. "George, Natalie, and I would sit down with whomever we were testing and just chitchat for a while, and then do a rehearsal at the table with a scene in the style of one that would be in *Episode II*, although it's not one that we'll see in the film. Then the actor and Natalie would rehearse and George would give notes. When everyone felt comfortable, we'd go to where we were shooting, do a blocking rehearsal, and then tape until George felt he had gotten what he wanted."

Choosing one of the final four was tough. Robin told *starwars.com*, "It's always a difficult

A Dream Come True

Natalie Portman will star with Hayden in *Star Wars Episode II: Attack of the Clones.*

process, but part of it is chemistry and how someone fits within an existing ensemble, and also how you picture his character as the future father of already established *Star Wars* characters [Luke Skywalker and Princess Leia Organa]."

HAYDEN CHRISTENSEN

George Lucas was impressed with Hayden. "He is very talented, has a great command of his craft, and I know he has the physical and emotional attributes to play Anakin Skywalker at perhaps the most complex stage of Anakin's life," Lucas told *starwars.com*.

Hayden's screen test revealed a lot about his personality to Robin. She told *starwars.com*, "Hayden has those special qualities you hope to find in an actor. He pops off the screen. And he had two of the characteristics that I was really seeking for the character of Anakin: He has vulnerability, and he has the edginess that's needed. We really had to have that combination, and it's rare to find an actor who can go back and forth so well."

It was important to Lucas to cast an unknown actor. He wanted audiences to see Hayden as Anakin from the moment he appeared onscreen. Producer Rick McCallum told *starwars.com*, "Everyone's excited, because I showed them

A Dream Come True

George Lucas is the creator of the *Star Wars* and *Indiana Jones* films.

some of the screen test. [Hayden's] really an unknown. I think the casting sends the signal that we're living by our word, and that we are anxiously working to deliver something new with this film."

A Dream Come True

FINDING OUT

Hayden was thrilled, yet stunned, to learn that he had gotten the part. "[During] the entire time I was involved in the casting process—for eight months—[the idea of] actually being in *Star Wars* seemed so far-fetched. When they told me I was going to the ranch [to audition], it became about meeting Natalie and just the thrill of shooting a scene from *Star Wars*. I figured I'd [just] get to walk away with some souvenirs, like a couple of hats," Hayden said in an interview with *USA Today*.

Of course, Hayden got more than just a couple of hats. The good news reached him early one morning. "I was just waking up and my roommate walked in and handed me the phone, and it was my agent and [my] manager, and they were pretty excited, so I knew as soon as I got on the phone," Hayden told *starwars.com*. But he couldn't tell anyone

Hayden's character is destined to become Darth Vader—one of the movies' most famous villains.

HAYDEN CHRISTENSEN

Lightsaber battles like this one made watching *Episode I* a thrilling experience for Hayden.

about it until it was officially announced. "I had this great secret I was so excited about, but I couldn't tell anybody," he explained to the *Toronto Sun*. "... I was always walking around with this big smile on my face and everyone was like, 'So, why are you so happy?' I was like, 'Yeaah, you'll find out soon enough.'"

A Dream Come True

"*Star Wars* has always been big for my generation," Hayden said on *starwars.com*. "When *Episode I* came out, my entire high school went to the theater for the first showing. It was a big event, and to be part of that now is very special."

Hayden's family was very happy when they learned he got the part. "I called my mom first thing, and my roommate started blaring the *Star Wars* soundtrack in the background," he told *starwars.com*. "I didn't want to tell my mom right off, but of course she heard the music and started flipping out."

JEDI KNIGHT IN TRAINING

Hayden spent many months studying and training for the role. The character of Anakin is faced with many challenges. First, he falls in love with Queen Amidala. Next, Anakin struggles with the dark side of the Force. Finally, he becomes the evil Darth Vader. But Hayden was not worried about learning the complicated

HAYDEN CHRISTENSEN

The road to love for Queen Amidala and Anakin Skywalker will be a bumpy one.

role. "It's awesome to portray a character who becomes Vader. I'm getting ready to go to the dark side," Hayden told *Time* magazine.

Hayden also had to get in shape to play a Jedi Knight. "As soon as he gets off the plane,

A Dream Come True

we'll be handing him over to [stunt coordinator] Nick Gillard for Jedi training. He'll be [working] flat out from the minute he gets [to Australia] until shooting," Rick McCallum told *starwars.com*.

To prepare for his battle scenes, Hayden took hours of fencing lessons. Learning to use a sword helped Hayden to properly use a lightsaber. Lightsabers are fictional weapons used by Jedi Knights in *Star Wars* movies. The lightsaber has a metal handle shaped like a cylinder. There are specially selected jewels and crystals within the handle that determine the color and length of the lightsaber's blade. With the push of a button, a long beam of powerful light extends from the handle. The beam of light is shaped like a sword blade. The lightsaber is very powerful. It can cut through almost anything except another lightsaber's beam.

After four weeks of training, Nick Gillard spoke with *starwars.com* about Hayden: "He's

HAYDEN CHRISTENSEN

The lightsaber is the Jedi Knights' weapon of choice.

fantastic. Not only is he a brilliant actor, but he has brilliant balance. He has all the ability; he's just so good. Hayden and Ewan [McGregor]

A Dream Come True

will both be doing all of their own stunts and swordfighting."

Hayden enjoyed his preparations to make the movie. He told *starwars.com*, "It's especially exciting to work with actors such as Natalie Portman and Ewan McGregor whom I've really admired. And I get to use lightsabers . . . and the Force!"

Luckily, Hayden was already an excellent athlete. He is an expert tennis player. In fact, he once planned to go to college on a tennis scholarship. He told *Entertainment Weekly*, "Dad wanted me to go to university on a tennis scholarship. When I got the part [in *Star Wars*], he sent me a card that said, 'Some things are bigger than a tennis scholarship to Harvard.'"

Hayden also enjoys playing hockey, in-line skating, skateboarding, and mountain biking. When he was working on "Higher Ground," he often did his own football stunts.

HAYDEN CHRISTENSEN

IN A GALAXY FAR, FAR AWAY

Star Wars gave Hayden his first opportunity to travel the world. *Episode II: Attack of the Clones* was filmed in Australia, Tunisia, and Italy. Before filming began, Hayden told *starwars.com*, "I've never been outside North America, so it will be an awesome way to see the world."

And before long, the world will be seeing a lot of Hayden as well. However, until *Episode II* is released in May 2002, the details of the story are being kept secret. George Lucas is determined to keep the script and the film footage under wraps until then. This means that Hayden and his co-stars Ewan McGregor (Obi-Wan Kenobi), Natalie Portman (Queen Amidala), and Samuel L. Jackson (Mace Windu) often did not get their scripts until the day of shooting.

A Dream Come True

Obi-Wan Kenobi, played by Ewan McGregor, becomes Anakin Skywalker's mentor.

NEW TECHNOLOGY
FOR THE NEW EPISODES

Star Wars Episode II: Attack of the Clones was shot with digital cameras instead of traditional film cameras. It will be the first major movie filmed entirely with digital cameras. *Episode III* will also use digital cameras.

The images recorded by a digital camera are saved onto a computer disk instead of film. Working with digital images on a disk makes adding special effects easier.

George Lucas gave a speech at the National Association of Broadcasters (NAB) 2001 Conference. He explained why he likes the digital camera better than the film camera: "The [digital] equipment is easier to use, and that allows you to get more angles and do more things than you'd normally be able to do. . . . The digital technology allows you to do an unlimited amount of changes and work in different ways that were not possible with the photo-chemical [film] process."

CHAPTER THREE

What the Future Holds

"Hayden is very talented. He just has this ability. I watch the show sometimes and I'm just kind of in awe of what he does. What comes across the screen is so beautiful and so true. It's incredible."
—"Higher Ground" co-star A.J. Cook in a *Toronto Sun* interview

The casting of Hayden as Anakin Skywalker made him an overnight celebrity. As soon as the news was announced, he was featured on the covers of both *Time* and *Entertainment Weekly*.

Hayden, seen here in a cast photo from "Higher Ground," is ready to take the leap into stardom.

HAYDEN CHRISTENSEN

A.J. Cook (center), seen here in a scene from *The Virgin Suicides*, worked with Hayden on this film and in "Higher Ground."

Not only will Hayden's face soon be on television and in magazines, it will also be seen on soda cans, posters, T-shirts, and action figures. As Anakin, Hayden will be instantly

What the Future Holds

recognized all over the world. So, will all of this fame go to his head? Not likely.

COPING WITH FAME

People have explained to Hayden that once his *Star Wars* movie is released, he could become a huge movie star. He told the *Toronto Sun*, "Of course, it's petrifying, especially coming from the position I was in prior to *Star Wars*. It'll be a change and, you know, you deal with it as it comes along and just hope you can cope."

Hayden has lots of family and friends to help him get through the glare of stardom. "I've got good people to talk to and to keep me grounded," he told the *Toronto Sun*. "I'll have my feet on the ground." With three siblings to keep an eye on him, Hayden will have a hard time getting a big head.

Matthew Hastings, the creator of "Higher Ground," thinks very highly of Hayden.

HAYDEN CHRISTENSEN

He knows Hayden is a good, decent guy. Matthew told the *Toronto Sun*, "He's become a very dear friend of mine. He is one of the most genuine and thoughtful people I know. He's soft-spoken, he's not arrogant, he's a really good, solid Canadian fellow. . . ."

A.J. Cook agrees. She told the *Toronto Star*, "He's a man of few words. Definitely, I think he'll shy away from a lot of [the attention] . . . . He's scared [and] he's nervous. He's a very private guy. I don't think he's going to be in . . . every single magazine. I think he'll hide away from [publicity] a lot."

That goes for his love life as well. Even though there have been rumors that he has dated his co-stars A.J. Cook and Natalie Portman, Hayden says little about his personal life.

BEYOND *STAR WARS*
After filming *Episode II*, Hayden appeared in another movie, *Life as a House*. It stars Kristin

What the Future Holds

Did you know?
Hayden received the "One to Watch" award at *Movieline's* third annual Young Hollywood Awards. The show was held at the House of Blues on Hollywood's Sunset Strip on April 29, 2001.

Scott Thomas (*The English Patient*), Kevin Kline (*The Wild, Wild West*), and Scott Bakula ("Enterprise"). The film is about a dying father trying to come to terms with his angry young son, played by Hayden. The film was written by Mark Andrus, who also wrote *As Good As It Gets*, a film that starred Jack Nicholson.

Hayden and his brother Tove are planning to

HAYDEN CHRISTENSEN

Movieline magazine named Hayden "One to Watch." Other winners of the honor were (left to right) Marissa Coughlan, Gabrielle Union, and Usher Raymond.

make a road-trip movie with Matthew Hastings called *Roadside Attractions*. And of course, Hayden will soon be preparing to star in *Star Wars: Episode III*, the final movie in the *Star Wars* prequel trilogy.

What the Future Holds

Despite his busy schedule, Hayden continues to do the things he likes best. He plays sports and hangs out with his friends. When he has time, he plays jazz and blues on the piano, even though he can't read music.

Hayden is grateful for the way his acting career has taken off. He hopes that his achievements will inspire other young actors to work toward their own acting goals.

He told the *Toronto Sun*, "I hope that, at the very least, [my success] inspires them to follow their dreams in acting . . . to take risks and to just get out there and do what you're going to do and not be afraid of whether you're going to be successful or not—because anything's possible . . . . I never would have thought that I'd be in *Star Wars*, and here I am."

For Hayden Christensen, it appears that the Force will be with him—*always!*

TIMELINE

1981 • Hayden Christensen is born in Vancouver, Canada, on April 19.

1994 • Hayden plays the part of Skip McDeere on the Canadian soap opera "Family Passions."

1995 • Hayden lands his first movie role, a paper boy in John Carpenter's *In the Mouth of Madness.*

1996 • Hayden plays Teddy Winfield in the TV movie *Danielle Steele's No Greater Love.*

1999 • Hayden has a small role in Sofia Coppola's *The Virgin Suicides*.
• Hayden joins the cast of the Fox Family Channel series "Higher Ground."

TIMELINE

2000
- "Higher Ground" runs for one season.
- Hayden gets the role of Anakin Skywalker in *Star Wars: Episode II* and *Episode III*.

2001
- Hayden stars in *Life as a House* with Kevin Kline and Kristin Scott Thomas.
- Hayden receives *Movieline's* "One to Watch" award.

2002
- *Star Wars Episode II: Attack of the Clones* hits theaters.

FACT SHEET

Name	Hayden Christensen
Born	April 19, 1981
Sign	Aries
Birthplace	Vancouver, British Columbia, Canada
Family	Father: David; Mother: Alie; Brother: Tove; Sisters: Hejsa and Kaylen
Hair	Blond
Height	6'4"
Eyes	Blue

Favorites

Food	Pizza
Color	Blue
Movie	*Star Wars Episode I: The Phantom Menace*
Sports	Tennis, hockey, in-line skating, mountain biking, beach-paddle tennis
Star Wars **Character**	Yoda

NEW WORDS

agent a person who finds jobs for actors, models, and musicians

audition a try-out performance for a role in a film or TV series

casting director a person who helps choose actors for roles in films and TV series

director the person who has artistic control of a film or TV series

ensemble a group

prequel a film or book whose story takes place before the story of another film or book

producer the person who supervises and raises money for a film or TV series

production company a company that makes films or TV shows

reviews critics opinions of performances or works of art

NEW WORDS

role the part played by an actor in a film or TV series

saga a long, detailed story of heroism

screen test a short film or video that helps determine whether an actor is right for a role

season a specific time of the year when a TV series airs

FOR FURTHER READING

Books
Rau, Dana Meachen and Christopher Rau. *George Lucas: Creator of Star Wars*. New York: Orchard Books, 1999.

Strasser, Todd. *Anakin Skywalker*. New York: Scholastic, 1999.

Watson, Jude. *Deceptions*. New York: Scholastic, 2001.

Wrede, Patricia C. *Star Wars Episode I: The Phantom Menace*. New York: Scholastic, 1999.

Magazines
Starlog
475 Park Avenue South
New York, NY 10016
www.starlog.com

Cinescape
12456 Ventura Blvd., Suite 2
Studio City, CA 91604
www.cinescape.com

RESOURCES

Web Sites
The Official Star Wars Web Site
http://www.starwars.com/
This is the official Web site for all of the *Star Wars* movies. Among its many features are cast, crew, and character bios, news updates on the making of *Episode II*, and video interviews. There are also trivia games and a photo gallery.

Internet Movie Database—Hayden Christensen
http://us.imdb.com/Name?Christensen, +Hayden
Check out Hayden's Internet Movie Database page. You can find information on all of his television and movie roles.

You can write to Hayden at:
Hayden Christensen
P.O. Box 5617
Beverly Hills, CA 90210

INDEX

A
agent, 7, 21
athlete, 27
audition, 15–16

C
casting director, 15
celebrity, 9, 33
Cook, A.J., 11, 36

D
director, 9, 15

E
ensemble, 17

F
"Family Passions," 8
fencing lessons, 25

G
Gurland, Robin, 15–16, 18

H
Hastings, Matthew, 35, 38
"Higher Ground," 9–11, 27, 35

J
Jackson, Samuel L., 28
Jedi Knight, 7, 15, 24–25

L
Life as a House, 36
Lucas, George, 15, 18, 28, 31

M
McGregor, Ewan, 27–28
music, 6, 23, 39

P
Portman, Natalie, 16, 27–28, 36
prequel, 13, 15–16, 38
producer, 18

INDEX

R
reviews, 11
Roadside Attractions, 38
role, 8–9, 13, 23–24

S
saga, 5
screen test, 16, 18–19
script, 28
season, 11

siblings, 6, 35
Skywalker, Anakin, 5, 13, 15, 18, 33
stunts, 27

T
trilogy, 13, 38

V
Vancouver, 6
Vader, Darth, 15, 23

ABOUT THE AUTHOR

Katherine Friedman was born in Los Angeles, California, but has lived in New York City since 1995. She received her M.F.A. in Creative Writing from New York University and works as a freelance writer. She is currently collaborating with a friend on a documentary film.